Be
PICTUR

Cookies, Cakes and Pies

GOLDEN PRESS/NEW YORK
Western Publishing Company, Inc.
Racine, Wisconsin

CONTENTS

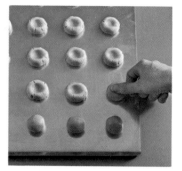

Press thumb firmly in center of each cookie before baking.

Store cookies plain. Fill as needed just before serving.

Peanut Butter Cookies

      1 cup sugar
      ½ cup butter or margarine, softened
      ½ cup peanut butter
      1 egg
      2 teaspoons vanilla
    1½ cups all-purpose flour*
      ½ teaspoon baking soda
      ½ teaspoon salt
      ½ teaspoon cream of tartar
      ½ teaspoon ground cinnamon
        About 7 tablespoons jelly

Heat oven to 350°. Mix sugar, butter, peanut butter, egg and vanilla until fluffy. Stir in flour, baking soda, salt, cream of tartar and cinnamon. Shape dough by teaspoonfuls into 1-inch balls. Place about 1½ inches apart on ungreased baking sheet; press thumb firmly in center of each.

Bake until set, 12 to 15 minutes. Remove from baking sheet; cool. Just before serving, fill center of each cookie with about ½ teaspoon of the jelly.   ABOUT 3½ DOZEN COOKIES.

*If using self-rising flour, omit baking soda and salt.

Peanut Butter Slices: Divide dough in half; refrigerate 1 hour. Shape each half into roll, 7x1½ inches; roll in 3 to 4 tablespoons chocolate shot. Wrap each roll in waxed paper; twist ends. Freeze about 1 hour.

Heat oven to 350°. Cut rolls into ⅛-inch slices. Place 1 inch apart on ungreased baking sheet. Bake until light brown, 8 to 10 minutes. Remove from baking sheet; cool. ABOUT 3 DOZEN SLICES.

Lemon-Spice Oatmeal Cookies

1 cup packed brown sugar
1 cup butter or margarine, softened
1 egg
1½ cups quick-cooking oats
1½ cups all-purpose flour*
1 cup chopped nuts
2 tablespoons grated lemon peel
½ teaspoon baking soda
½ teaspoon salt
½ teaspoon ground cinnamon
¼ teaspoon ground cloves
¼ teaspoon ground allspice
Lemon Glaze (below)

Heat oven to 375°. Mix brown sugar, butter and egg thoroughly. Stir in oats, flour, nuts, lemon peel, baking soda, salt, cinnamon, cloves and allspice. Shape dough by tablespoonfuls into 1½-inch balls. Place 1 inch apart on ungreased baking sheet; press down with fork. Bake until almost no indentation remains when touched, 8 to 10 minutes. Cool slightly; remove from baking sheet. Spread Lemon Glaze over cookies. Cool completely. ABOUT 2½ DOZEN COOKIES.

*If using self-rising flour, omit baking soda and salt.

LEMON GLAZE
Mix 1 cup powdered sugar, 2 tablespoons lemon juice and 2 teaspoons butter or margarine, softened, until smooth.

Shape the dough into balls.

Press down balls with fork.

Half-Moon Cookies

2 cups quick-cooking oats
1 cup packed brown sugar
½ cup vegetable oil
1 egg
½ teaspoon almond extract
¼ teaspoon salt
1 package (6 ounces) semisweet chocolate
   chips

Heat oven to 325°. Mix oats, brown sugar and oil until well blended. Stir in egg, extract and salt. Drop mixture by teaspoonfuls 1½ inches apart onto lightly greased baking sheet. Bake until brown around edges, 10 to 15 minutes. Cool; remove from baking sheet.

Heat chocolate chips in 1-quart saucepan over low heat until melted, stirring constantly. Frost half of each cookie as pictured; cool on wire rack. After chocolate is set, refrigerate between sheets of waxed paper about 30 minutes.
3 DOZEN COOKIES.

SHELF SERVICE

Store cereals, pasta, rice, crackers and dry bread crumbs in tightly closed containers in a cool, dry place away from soaps or foods with strong odors. For maximum flavor, store pasta (except egg noodles) and white rice up to 1 year; dry bread crumbs, egg noodles and brown or wild rice 6 months; cornmeal, oatmeal and hominy grits 4 to 6 months; crackers and ready-to-eat cereals 3 months. To re-crisp cereal, place it in a shallow baking pan in a 350° oven for about 5 minutes.

Oatmeal Drops

1½ cups quick-cooking oats
 ½ cup sugar
  3 tablespoons butter or margarine, softened
  1 teaspoon vanilla
 ½ teaspoon baking powder
 ½ teaspoon ground cinnamon
 ¼ teaspoon salt
  1 egg

Heat oven to 350°. Mix all ingredients. Drop dough by teaspoonfuls 2 inches apart onto greased baking sheet. Bake
until tops are dry and edges are light brown, 8 to 10
minutes. Cool slightly; remove from baking sheet.
3 DOZEN COOKIES.

Cereal Crisps

  2 eggs
  1 cup sugar
  2 cups chocolate-flavored corn puff cereal
  1 cup all-purpose flour
1½ teaspoons vanilla
 ½ teaspoon ground nutmeg
 ¼ teaspoon ground cardamom
 ⅛ teaspoon salt

Heat oven to 375°. Beat eggs until very thick. Beat in sugar
until well mixed. Stir in remaining ingredients. Refrigerate
until dough is stiff, about 15 minutes.

Drop dough by teaspoonfuls 2 inches apart onto greased
baking sheet. Bake until edges are light brown, 10 to 12
minutes. Immediately remove from baking sheet. Cool on
wire rack.   4 DOZEN COOKIES.

Stir in flour, soda, salt, oats and chocolate-covered raisins.

Drop dough by rounded tea-spoonfuls onto baking sheet.

Raisin Cookies

- 1 cup packed brown sugar
- ½ cup shortening
- 1 egg
- 3 tablespoons water
- 1½ teaspoons vanilla
- 1 cup all-purpose flour*
- ½ teaspoon baking soda
- ½ teaspoon salt
- 1½ cups quick-cooking oats
- 1¾ cups chocolate-covered raisins (about 12 ounces)

Heat oven to 350°. Beat brown sugar, shortening, egg, water and vanilla until light and fluffy. Stir in flour, baking soda, salt, oats and chocolate-covered raisins. Drop dough by rounded teaspoonfuls 2 inches apart onto ungreased baking sheet. Bake until light brown, about 10 minutes.

ABOUT 4 DOZEN COOKIES.

*If using self-rising flour, omit baking soda and salt.

Soft Cocoa Drops

⅓ cup sugar
¼ cup cocoa
3 eggs, separated
¾ cup all-purpose flour*
¼ teaspoon baking powder
¼ teaspoon ground cinnamon
⅛ teaspoon salt
¼ cup water
1 teaspoon vanilla
¼ teaspoon lemon extract
¼ teaspoon cream of tartar
¼ cup sugar

Heat oven to 350°. Grease and flour 2 baking sheets. Beat ⅓ cup sugar, the cocoa and egg yolks in small mixer bowl on medium speed until very thick, about 3 minutes. Beat in flour, baking powder, cinnamon and salt alternately with water, vanilla and lemon extract on low speed.

Beat egg whites and cream of tartar in large mixer bowl until foamy. Beat in ¼ cup sugar gradually; continue beating until stiff and glossy. Fold egg yolk mixture into egg whites. Drop by rounded tablespoonfuls 2 inches apart onto baking sheets. Bake until set, 10 to 12 minutes.
30 COOKIES.

*If using self-rising flour, omit baking powder and salt.

NOTE-ABLE KITCHEN GIFTS

For a special touch, when you give a gift of food from your "kitchen boutique," include a copy of your recipe. List all menu suggestions and serving tips, too. Label all gifts that require refrigeration and if there is a specific storage time or additonal preparation information (reheating, baking, etc.), be sure to note it on your label as well.

Sesame Bars

4 packages (2⅜ ounces each) sesame seed
1 cup butter or margarine, softened
2 cups packed brown sugar
2 eggs, beaten
1 cup all-purpose flour*
2 tablespoons hot water
¾ teaspoon salt

Heat oven to 325°. Mix all ingredients. Spread in greased jelly roll pan, 15½x10½x1 inch. Bake until center is set, 45 minutes. Cool; cut into bars, 2x1 inch.   6 DOZEN BARS.

*Do not use self-rising flour in this recipe.

Slice the almond paste; chop the slices into small pieces.

With knife point down, move handle in circle to chop nuts.

Almond Brownies

    4 squares (1 ounce each) unsweetened
       chocolate
 ⅔ cup shortening
    2 cups sugar
    4 eggs
1¼ cups all-purpose flour*
    1 teaspoon baking powder
    1 teaspoon salt
    1 cup chopped nuts
    1 cup chopped almond paste

Heat oven to 350°. Grease baking pan, 13x9x2 inches. Heat chocolate and shortening in 3-quart saucepan over low heat until melted; remove from heat. Stir in remaining ingredients. Spread in pan.

Bake until brownies begin to pull away from sides of pan, about 30 minutes. Do not overbake. Cool slightly; cut into bars, about 2x1½ inches.   ABOUT 3 DOZEN BARS.

*If using self-rising flour, omit baking powder and salt.

Press butter mixture firmly and evenly in baking pan.

Beat the eggs, brown sugar and vanilla until foamy.

Stir the coconut and almonds into the flour mixture.

Spread mixture evenly over crust; bake 25 minutes.

Frosted Lemon Bars

½ cup butter or margarine, softened
½ cup packed brown sugar
 1 cup all-purpose flour
 2 eggs
 1 cup packed brown sugar
 1 teaspoon vanilla
¼ cup all-purpose flour*
 1 teaspoon baking powder
 1 teaspoon grated lemon peel
½ teaspoon salt
 1 cup flaked coconut
½ cup chopped almonds
   Lemon Frosting (below)

Heat oven to 350°. Mix butter and ½ cup brown sugar; stir in 1 cup flour. Press mixture firmly and evenly in ungreased baking pan, 13x9x2 inches. Bake 10 minutes.

Beat eggs, 1 cup brown sugar and the vanilla until foamy. Beat in ¼ cup flour, the baking powder, lemon peel and salt on low speed. Stir in coconut and almonds; spread over crust. Bake 25 minutes. Cool completely. Frost with Lemon Frosting. Cut into bars, 3x1 inch.   3 DOZEN BARS.

*If using self-rising flour, omit baking powder and salt.

LEMON FROSTING

Mix 2 cups powdered sugar, 1 teaspoon grated lemon peel, 2 teaspoons lemon juice and about 2 tablespoons milk until smooth and of spreading consistency.

Blend cake mix, peanut butter and sugar until crumbly; reserve ⅔ cup of crumb mixture.

Stir the nuts into the reserved crumb mixture; sprinkle evenly over the batter in pan.

Peanut Butter Bars

---

    1 package (18.5 ounces) yellow cake mix
    1 cup crunchy peanut butter
    ½ cup packed brown sugar
    2 eggs
    ⅓ cup water
    ¼ cup shortening
    1 package (12 ounces) semisweet chocolate chips
    ⅔ cup chopped nuts

Heat oven to 350°. Grease and flour jelly roll pan, 15½x10½x1 inch. Blend cake mix (dry), peanut butter and brown sugar in large mixer bowl on low speed until crumbly. Reserve ⅔ cup of the crumb mixture.

Blend remaining crumb mixture, the eggs, water and shortening on low speed until moistened, scraping bowl constantly. Beat on medium speed 2 minutes, scraping bowl occasionally. Stir in chocolate chips. Spread batter in pan.

Stir nuts into reserved crumb mixture; sprinkle over batter. Bake until set, about 25 minutes. Cool until firm. Cut into 3x1½-inch bars.   30 BARS.

16

Chip 'n Granola Bars

⅓ cup shortening
⅓ cup butter or margarine
½ cup granulated sugar
½ cup packed brown sugar
1 egg
1 teaspoon vanilla
1½ cups all-purpose flour*
½ teaspoon baking soda
½ teaspoon salt
1 package (6 ounces) semisweet chocolate chips
1 cup granola (any flavor)

Heat oven to 375°. Grease baking pan, 13x9x2 inches. Mix shortening, butter, sugars, egg and vanilla thoroughly. Stir in remaining ingredients. Spread dough in pan. Bake until light brown, 20 to 25 minutes. Cut into 3x1½-inch bars. 2 DOZEN BARS.

*If using self-rising flour, omit baking soda and salt.

Chip 'n Nut Bars: Substitute 1 package (4 ounces) shelled sunflower nuts for the granola.

Add the chocolate chips and granola to shortening mixture.

Spread the dough evenly in a greased baking pan.

The Cookie Mix (16 cups) is made from these ingredients.

First mix in 2 cups of the mix, then add remaining 2 cups.

Cookie Mix

8 cups all-purpose flour*
2 cups packed brown sugar
2 cups granulated sugar
1 tablespoon salt
1½ teaspoons baking soda
1½ cups shortening

Mix flour, brown sugar, granulated sugar, salt and baking soda. Cut in shortening completely until particles are size of coarse cornmeal. (Be sure brown sugar is blended.) Refrigerate in airtight container up to 1 month.   16 CUPS MIX.

*If using self-rising flour, omit salt and baking soda.

Cherry-Nut Drops

4 cups Cookie Mix (above)
1 egg, beaten
⅔ cup coarsely chopped maraschino cherries
½ cup chopped nuts
1 tablespoon water

Heat oven to 350°. Mix 2 cups of the Cookie Mix and the remaining ingredients. Stir in remaining Cookie Mix gradually until mix is moistened. Drop dough by teaspoonfuls 2 inches apart onto ungreased baking sheet. Bake until light brown around edges, 12 to 15 minutes.   4 DOZEN COOKIES.

Buttery Cookies

⅓ cup butter or margarine, softened
1 egg yolk
2½ cups Cookie Mix (page 19)
   Sugar
   Pecan halves

Heat oven to 350°. Mix butter and egg yolk; stir in Cookie Mix until smooth. Shape dough into 1-inch balls. Place 3 inches apart on ungreased baking sheet. Flatten balls with bottom of glass dipped in sugar. Press pecan half into each cookie. Bake until light brown, 12 to 15 minutes.
2½ DOZEN COOKIES.

Spread the dough for Cashew Bars in greased baking pan.

Sprinkle cashews over dough; press lightly onto surface.

Cashew Bars

2½ cups Cookie Mix (page 19)
  1 egg, beaten
  2 tablespoons butter or margarine, softened
 ½ teaspoon baking powder
  1 teaspoon vanilla
 ½ cup broken cashews

Heat oven to 350°. Mix Cookie Mix, egg, butter, baking powder and vanilla until smooth. Spread dough in greased baking pan, 9x9x2 inches. Sprinkle cashews over dough; press lightly onto surface. Bake 20 minutes. Cool; cut into bars, about 2x1½ inches.   2 DOZEN BARS.

Granola

4 cups quick-cooking oats
1 cup chopped salted peanuts
1 cup dry roasted sunflower nuts
1 cup unsweetened shredded or sweetened
  flaked coconut
⅔ cup light corn syrup
⅓ cup vegetable oil
1½ cups golden raisins

Heat oven to 300°. Mix oats, peanuts, sunflower nuts and coconut in large bowl. Mix corn syrup and oil; pour on oats mixture, stirring until coated completely. Spread in lightly greased jelly roll pan, 15½x10½x1 inch. Bake, stirring every 15 minutes, 1 hour. Stir in raisins; cool. 8 CUPS GRANOLA.

Lemon Ice Bars

1 cup packed brown sugar
¼ cup butter or margarine, softened
2 eggs, slightly beaten
1 teaspoon vanilla
1 cup all-purpose flour*
½ teaspoon baking powder
½ teaspoon salt
1 cup Granola (above)
⅓ cup chopped maraschino cherries, drained
  Lemon Ice (right)
  Maraschino cherries, cut into fourths and
    drained

Heat oven to 350°. Beat brown sugar, butter, eggs and vanilla until fluffy. Stir in flour, baking powder and salt until flour is moistened. Stir in Granola and chopped cherries. Pour into greased baking pan, 9x9x2 inches. Bake until wooden pick inserted in center comes out clean, 30 to 35 minutes. Cool completely on wire rack. Frost with Lemon Ice. Cut into bars, about 2x1½ inches. Decorate with cut cherries.   2 DOZEN BARS.

'If using self-rising flour, omit baking powder and salt.

LEMON ICE
⅔ cup powdered sugar
1 tablespoon to 1 tablespoon plus 1½
   teaspoons lemon juice
1 tablespoon butter or margarine, softened
1 teaspoon grated lemon peel

Beat all ingredients until smooth and creamy.

Cherry-Fudge Cake

---

    2 cups all-purpose flour*
    2 cups sugar
    1 cup water
  ¾ cup dairy sour cream
  ¼ cup shortening
1¼ teaspoons baking soda
    1 teaspoon salt
    1 teaspoon almond extract
  ½ teaspoon baking powder
    2 eggs
    4 squares (1 ounce each) unsweetened
       chocolate, melted and cooled
       Chocolate-Cherry Frosting (right)

Heat oven to 350°. Grease and flour baking pan, 13x9x2 inches. Mix all ingredients except Chocolate-Cherry Frosting on low speed 30 seconds, scraping bowl constantly. Beat on high speed 3 minutes, scraping bowl occasionally; pour into pan. Bake until top springs back when touched lightly, 40 to 45 minutes. Cool. Frost with Chocolate-Cherry Frosting.

*If using self-rising flour, reduce baking soda to ¼ teaspoon and omit salt and baking powder.

CHOCOLATE-CHERRY FROSTING
Drain 1 jar (10 ounces) maraschino cherries, reserving ½ cup syrup. Chop cherries; drain on paper towels. Arrange cherries on cake. Mix reserved syrup and 2 envelopes (1 ounce each) premelted unsweetened chocolate in small mixer bowl. Beat in 3 cups powdered sugar until smooth. Pour frosting on cherries carefully; spread frosting to cover cake.

Arrange chopped cherries on top of the cooled cake.

Pour frosting on cherries; spread to cover the cake.

Fudgy Chocolate Cake

1 cup butter or margarine
1 cup water
½ cup cocoa
2 cups all-purpose flour*
2 cups sugar
½ cup dairy sour cream
2 eggs
1 teaspoon baking soda
½ teaspoon salt
  Butter Frosting (below)

Heat oven to 350°. Grease and flour baking pan, 13x9x2 inches. Heat butter, water and cocoa to boiling in 3-quart saucepan, stirring occasionally. Remove from heat. Add flour, sugar, sour cream, eggs, baking soda and salt. Beat on medium speed or with hand beater until smooth, about 2 minutes. Pour into pan. Bake until wooden pick inserted in center comes out clean, 35 to 40 minutes. Cool completely. Frost with Butter Frosting.

*If using self-rising flour, omit baking soda and salt.

BUTTER FROSTING

⅓ cup butter or margarine, softened
3 cups powdered sugar
1 teaspoon orange flavoring or allspice
2 to 3 tablespoons milk

Mix butter, sugar and flavoring until thoroughly blended. Stir in milk; beat until frosting is smooth and of spreading consistency.

Irish Chocolate Cake: Substitute 2 teaspoons Irish whiskey and 1 to 2 teaspoons instant coffee for the orange flavoring in the frosting.

Heat butter, water and cocoa to boiling in 3-quart saucepan, stirring occasionally.

Remove from heat. Add flour, sugar, sour cream, eggs, soda and salt; beat until smooth.

Fold flour mixture ¼ cup at a time into the meringue, turning the bowl as you fold.

Gently cut through batter to break any air pockets and seal the batter to pan.

Bake until top of cake springs back when touched lightly and the cracks feel dry.

Invert pan to let cake cool. (If cake falls out of pan, it has been underbaked.)

Caramel-Orange Angel Cake

1¼ cups cake flour
 1 cup packed brown sugar
 12 egg whites (about 1½ cups)
1½ teaspoons cream of tartar
 1 teaspoon salt
 1 cup packed brown sugar
 3 teaspoons shredded orange peel
1½ teaspoons vanilla
 3 cups frozen whipped topping, thawed

Heat oven to 375°. Mix flour and 1 cup brown sugar. Beat egg whites, cream of tartar and salt in large bowl until foamy. Beat in 1 cup brown sugar, 2 tablespoons at a time, on high speed until stiff peaks form; sprinkle with 2 teaspoons of the orange peel and the vanilla.

Fold flour mixture, ¼ cup at a time, into meringue as pictured just until flour mixture disappears. Spread batter in ungreased tube pan, 10x4 inches. Gently cut through batter with knife. Bake until top springs back when touched lightly and cracks are dry, 30 to 35 minutes.

Invert pan on funnel as pictured; let hang until cake is cool. Frost cake with whipped topping. Sprinkle with remaining orange peel. Refrigerate until serving time.

HOW TO FOLD ANGEL CAKES

Sprinkle flour mixture over egg white meringue. Fold by cutting down through the center of meringue, along the bottom and up the side. Rotate bowl ¼ turn; repeat. Not all of the flour mixture disappears with each folding motion. Continue folding just until the flour mixture disappears. Too much folding breaks down the cake.

Carnival Ice-Cream Cake

   One 10-inch round angel food cake
1 envelope (.24 ounce) strawberry-flavored
     unsweetened soft drink mix
1 envelope (.24 ounce) orange-flavored
     unsweetened soft drink mix
1 envelope (.24 ounce) raspberry-flavored
     unsweetened soft drink mix
1 package (10 ounces) frozen sliced
     strawberries, thawed
½ gallon vanilla ice cream, slightly softened
1 package (10 ounces) frozen sliced peaches,
     thawed and cut up
1 package (10 ounces) frozen raspberries,
     thawed

Tear cake into bite-size pieces. Divide among 3 bowls. Sprinkle strawberry drink mix over cake in 1 bowl, orange over the second and raspberry over the third. Toss each lightly with fork until cake pieces are well coated with drink mix.

Line 10-inch tube pan with aluminum foil. Place strawberry cake pieces in pan; spoon strawberries (with liquid) onto cake. Spread ⅓ of the ice cream over strawberries. Repeat layers with orange cake pieces, peaches (with liquid), half of the remaining ice cream, the raspberry cake pieces, raspberries (with liquid) and remaining ice cream. Cover and freeze 24 hours.

About 2 hours before serving, place cake in refrigerator. About 30 minutes before serving, unmold on chilled plate; remove aluminum foil. Refrigerate until serving time.
16 TO 20 SERVINGS.

Toss cake pieces with drink mix. Place layer of strawberry cake pieces, strawberries and ice cream in pan.

Repeat with orange cake pieces, peaches, ice cream, then raspberry cake pieces, raspberries and remaining ice cream.

To make topping, refrigerate maple syrup mixture until it mounds when dropped.

Beat the chilled maple syrup mixture on high speed until fluffy and stiff peaks form.

Maple Angel

1 package (15 ounces) traditional angel food
   cake mix
½ cup low-calorie maple-flavored syrup
3 tablespoons nonfat dry milk
1 teaspoon unflavored gelatin
½ teaspoon vanilla

Prepare cake mix as directed on package. Heat syrup, dry milk and gelatin over medium heat, stirring constantly, until gelatin is dissolved, about 3 minutes. Stir in vanilla. Pour into small mixer bowl. Refrigerate until mixture mounds slightly when dropped from a spoon, about 30 minutes.

Cut cake into 16 servings. Beat syrup mixture on high speed until stiff peaks form. Spoon 2 tablespoons topping onto each serving.　16 SERVINGS.

Green Angel

Prepare 1 package (16 ounces) one-step white angel food cake mix as directed except—substitute 1 can (12 ounces) sugar-free lemon-lime-flavored carbonated beverage and 4 drops green food color for the cold water.   16 SERVINGS.

Pastel Angels: Substitute 1 can (12 ounces) sugar-free orange-, strawberry- or grape-flavored carbonated beverage for the lemon-lime-flavored beverage. Omit food color and stir in 1 to 2 teaspoons grated lemon peel.

Minted Angel Allegretti

- 1 package (15 or 16 ounces) white angel food cake mix
- 2¼ cups miniature marshmallows
- ½ cup milk
- ¼ cup white or green crème de menthe
- ¼ teaspoon salt
- 4 to 6 drops green food color
- 1 pint chilled whipping cream
- 1 packet (1 ounce) premelted unsweetened chocolate (see note)

Bake cake mix as directed on package. Cool. Split cake to make 3 layers.

Heat marshmallows and milk over medium heat, stirring occasionally, until marshmallows are melted, about 5 minutes; remove from heat. Cool at room temperature until thickened, 20 to 25 minutes. Stir in crème de menthe, salt and food color.

Beat whipping cream in chilled small mixer bowl until stiff peaks form. Fold into marshmallow mixture. Stack cake layers, spreading top of each with 1 cup of the filling. Frost side of cake with remaining filling. Drizzle chocolate around top edge of cake, allowing it to run down side; refrigerate until serving time.   ABOUT 16 SERVINGS.

Note: To soften chocolate, place packet in bowl of warm water.

To split cake, mark evenly with picks. Using picks as a guide, cut across cake.

Cool marshmallow mixture at room temperature just until it is slightly thickened.

For frosting, stir milk into cooked butter-sugar mixture.

Beat powdered sugar into the cooled frosting; add cashews.

Butterscotch Nut Cake

    1 cup all-purpose flour*
    1 cup whole wheat flour
    1 cup packed brown sugar
    ½ cup granulated sugar
    3½ teaspoons baking powder
    1 teaspoon salt
    ½ cup shortening
    1 cup milk
    1 teaspoon vanilla
    3 eggs
      Cashew Frosting (right)

Heat oven to 350°. Grease and flour baking pan, 13x9x2 inches. Blend all ingredients except Cashew Frosting on low speed 30 seconds, scraping bowl constantly. Beat on high speed 3 minutes, scraping bowl occasionally; pour into pan. Bake until pick inserted in center comes out clean, 40 to 45 minutes. Cool. Frost with Cashew Frosting.

*If using self-rising flour, omit baking powder and salt.

CASHEW FROSTING

- ½ cup butter or margarine
- ¾ cup packed brown sugar
- ¼ cup milk
- 2 cups powdered sugar
- ½ cup broken cashews

Heat butter in 2-quart saucepan until melted. Stir in brown sugar. Heat to boiling, stirring constantly; reduce heat. Boil and stir 2 minutes. Stir in milk; heat to boiling. Cool. Beat in powdered sugar gradually; continue beating until of spreading consistency. Stir in cashews.

Mocha Revel Cake

```
    1  cup packed brown sugar
    ½  cup all-purpose flour
    ⅓  cup cocoa
    ¼  cup butter or margarine, softened
    1  package (18.5 ounces) yellow cake mix
 1¼  cups water
    ¼  cup vegetable oil
    1  tablespoon instant coffee
    3  eggs
       Cocoa Glaze (right)
```

Heat oven to 350°. Grease generously and flour 12-cup bundt cake pan. Mix brown sugar, flour, cocoa and butter until crumbly; reserve. Blend cake mix (dry), water, oil, coffee and eggs on low speed until moistened; beat 4 minutes on medium speed. Pour half of the batter (about 2 cups) into pan; sprinkle with half of the reserved cocoa mixture (about 1⅓ cups). Repeat, using half of the remaining batter, the remaining cocoa mixture and remaining batter. Bake until cake springs back when touched lightly in center, 45 to 50 minutes. Cool cake 10 minutes; remove from pan. Cool completely. Spread cake with Cocoa Glaze.

COCOA GLAZE
1 tablespoon butter or margarine
2 tablespoons cocoa
1 tablespoon water
1 cup powdered sugar
2 to 4 teaspoons water

Heat butter until melted. Stir in cocoa and 1 tablespoon water until smooth; remove from heat. Stir in sugar and enough water to reach desired glaze consistency.

Sprinkle batter in cake pan with half of the cocoa mixture.

Pour half of the remaining batter on the cocoa mixture.

For the glaze, add cocoa and water to the melted butter.

Glaze should be thin enough to drizzle down side of cake.

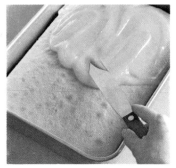

Spread cooled lemon filling evenly over cake.

Add nutmeg to the frosting mix before beating.

Lemon Meringue Cake

1 package (18.5 ounces) yellow cake mix
1 tablespoon grated lemon peel
   Lemon Filling (below)
1 package (7.2 ounces) fluffy white frosting
   mix
¼ teaspoon ground nutmeg (optional)

Prepare cake mix as directed on package except—add lemon peel before beating. Bake in 13x9x2-inch pan as directed. Cool.

Prepare Lemon Filling; reserve ⅓ cup. Spread remaining filling over cake. Prepare frosting mix as directed on package except—add nutmeg before beating. Frost cake. Swirl reserved filling on frosting or make lattice design. (Thin reserved filling with small amount of water if necessary.)

LEMON FILLING
   1 cup sugar
   ¼ cup cornstarch
   ¼ teaspoon salt
   1 cup water
   ⅓ cup lemon juice
   2 tablespoons butter or margarine
1½ teaspoons grated lemon peel
   4 to 6 drops yellow food color (optional)

Mix sugar, cornstarch and salt in 1-quart saucepan. Stir in water gradually. Cook over medium heat, stirring constantly, until mixture thickens and boils. Boil and stir 1 minute; remove from heat. Stir in remaining ingredients. Cool completely. If filling is too soft, refrigerate until set.

Do-Ahead Coconut Pound Cake

2¾ cups sugar
1¼ cups butter or margarine, softened
  5 eggs
  1 teaspoon vanilla
  3 cups all-purpose flour*
  1 teaspoon baking powder
  ¼ teaspoon salt
  1 cup evaporated milk
  1 can (3½ ounces) flaked coconut
  2 to 3 tablespoons shredded orange peel

Heat oven to 350°. Grease and flour tube pan, 10x4 inches, or 12-cup bundt cake pan. Blend sugar, butter, eggs and vanilla in large mixer bowl ½ minute on low speed, scraping bowl constantly. Beat 5 minutes on high speed, scraping bowl occasionally. On low speed, mix in flour, baking powder and salt alternately with milk. Fold in coconut and orange peel. Pour into pan. Bake until wooden pick inserted in center comes out clean, 1 to 1¼ hours.

Cool 20 minutes; remove from pan. Cool completely. Serve immediately or wrap and refrigerate or freeze. Store in refrigerator up to 1 week, in freezer up to 4 months.

■2 hours before serving, remove cake from freezer and loosen wrapper so that it does not touch cake. Thaw at room temperature.

*Do not use self-rising flour in this recipe.

Almond Pound Cake: Substitute almond extract for the vanilla and sprinkle 1 package (1½ ounces) sliced almonds (about ¼ cup) on batter before baking; omit coconut.

Lemon Pound Cake: Substitute lemon extract for the vanilla and 2 to 3 teaspoons finely grated lemon peel for the orange peel. Omit coconut.

Tap and shake flour in the pan to cover it completely.

Mix in the milk alternately with the dry ingredients.

Oven rack should be placed below the center of oven.

Bake until pick inserted in the center comes out clean.

You need these ingredients to make the Cake Mix (13 cups).

Place rack on top of cake; invert. Lift pan off cake; cool.

Cake Mix

Mix 9 cups all-purpose flour,* ⅓ cup baking powder, ¼ cup sugar, 1 tablespoon salt and 1 teaspoon baking soda. Cut in 2 cups shortening completely until particles are size of coarse cornmeal. Refrigerate in airtight container up to 1 month.   13 CUPS MIX.

*Do not use self-rising flour in this recipe.

Golden Orange Cake

3	cups Cake Mix (above)
1¼	cups buttermilk
¾	cup sugar
1	teaspoon baking soda
3	tablespoons butter or margarine, softened
3	eggs
1	tablespoon grated orange peel
1	teaspoon vanilla
⅔	cup golden raisins, cut up
⅓	cup chopped walnuts
	Orange Glaze (below)

Heat oven to 350°. Grease and flour 9-cup bundt cake pan or baking pan, 13x9x2 inches. Beat Cake Mix, buttermilk, sugar, baking soda, butter, eggs, orange peel and vanilla in large mixer bowl on low speed, scraping bowl constantly, 30 seconds. Beat on medium speed, scraping bowl occasionally, 4 minutes. Beat in raisins and walnuts. Bake until wooden pick inserted in center comes out clean, 50 to 55 minutes. Remove from pan; cool. Drizzle with glaze.

ORANGE GLAZE
Mix 3 tablespoons butter or margarine, melted, 1 cup powdered sugar and 2 teaspoons grated orange peel. Stir in 1 to 2 tablespoons orange juice until of desired consistency.

Sacher Torte

---

    3 cups Cake Mix (page 45)
1½ cups sugar
    ½ cup cocoa
1¼ cups milk
    ⅓ cup butter or margarine, softened
    2 eggs, slightly beaten
    1 teaspoon vanilla
1½ cups apricot preserves
       Chocolate Glaze (right)

Heat oven to 350°. Grease and flour 2 round layer pans, 9x1½ inches. Mix Cake Mix, sugar and cocoa in large mixer bowl. Beat in milk, butter, eggs and vanilla on low speed, scraping bowl constantly, 30 seconds. Beat on medium speed, scraping bowl occasionally, 4 minutes. Pour into pans. Bake until wooden pick inserted in center comes out clean, 24 to 30 minutes. Cool no longer than 10 minutes. Remove from pan; cool completely.

Split to make 4 layers; fill layers with apricot preserves. Spread top and side with Chocolate Glaze.

CHOCOLATE GLAZE

**3 ounces unsweetened chocolate, broken into
  pieces**
1 cup sugar
1 cup whipping cream
1 teaspoon light corn syrup
2 egg yolks, slightly beaten
1 teaspoon vanilla

Heat chocolate, sugar, cream and corn syrup over medium heat, stirring constantly, until chocolate is melted; reduce heat. Simmer, without stirring, 10 minutes. Stir 2 tablespoons chocolate mixture, 1 teaspoon at a time, into egg yolks; stir into chocolate mixture in pan. Cook over low heat, stirring constantly, until mixture coats a spoon, 3 to 4 minutes. Stir in vanilla. Cool to room temperature.

Split each layer in half, using a long, thin, sharp knife and wooden picks as a guide.

Fill 3 cake layers with apricot preserves, then add the fourth layer, rounded side up.

Drizzle glaze over top and side. Waxed paper strips keep plate clean as you frost.

Spread top and side of torte with Chocolate Glaze, bringing the glaze up the side.

Carefully fold chocolate mixture into beaten egg whites.

Fill pie plate with chocolate mixture until level with edge.

As baked pie cools, it sinks in the center to form a shell.

Without stirring, fill shell with the reserved filling.

Mocha Fudge Pie

- ¼ cup graham cracker crumbs (about 3 squares)
- ½ cup water
- 2 teaspoons instant coffee
- ⅛ teaspoon salt
- 8 eggs, separated
- 2 packages (4 ounces each) sweet cooking chocolate, broken into pieces
- 1 teaspoon brandy flavoring
- ½ cup sugar
- ¾ cup chilled whipping cream
- 2 tablespoons sugar
  Chocolate curls

Butter 8-inch pie plate; sprinkle with crumbs. Mix water, instant coffee and salt in 2-quart saucepan. Beat egg yolks slightly; stir egg yolks and chocolate pieces into coffee mixture. Cook over medium heat, stirring constantly, until mixture thickens but does not boil, 6 to 8 minutes. Remove from heat; stir in flavoring. Cool.

Heat oven to 350°. Beat egg whites in large mixer bowl until foamy. Beat in ½ cup sugar, 1 tablespoon at a time; continue beating until stiff and glossy. Fold chocolate mixture into egg whites carefully, without stirring. Fill pie plate with chocolate mixture until level with edge. Cover and refrigerate remaining chocolate mixture. Bake pie 25 minutes.

Turn off oven; leave pie in oven with door closed 5 minutes. Remove from oven; cool on wire rack 2 hours. As chocolate mixture cools, it sinks in the center to form a pie shell. Fill shell with chilled chocolate mixture. Refrigerate until chilled, at least 2 hours.

Beat whipping cream and 2 tablespoons sugar in chilled small mixer bowl until stiff. Spread whipped cream evenly over pie. Garnish with chocolate curls.   6 TO 8 SERVINGS.

Cool Mint Cookie Pie

½ cup nonfat dry milk
½ cup iced water
2 egg whites
1 teaspoon lemon juice
¼ cup sugar
¼ teaspoon peppermint extract
5 drops green food color
⅓ cup small pastel pillow mints
1 chocolate wafer, finely crushed (about
 1 tablespoon)

Beat dry milk, water and egg whites in small mixer bowl on high speed 3 minutes. Beat in lemon juice on high speed 1 minute. Beat in sugar, 1 tablespoon at a time; continue beating until thick and fluffy, about 2 minutes (do not over-beat). Beat in extract and food color until well mixed, about 15 seconds. Fold in mints; pour into ungreased 9-inch pie plate. Sprinkle with wafer crumbs. Freeze uncovered until firm, about 1 hour.

To make filling thick and fluffy, use an electric mixer.

Fold in pastel pillow mints; pour into 9-inch pie plate.

To make crust, press coconut into buttered pie plate; bake.

Spread filling in cooled pie crust. Refrigerate until set.

Jeweled Fruit Pie

Toasted Coconut Crust (below)
1 can (14 ounces) sweetened condensed milk
⅓ cup lemon juice
1 can (8¾ ounces) fruit cocktail, drained
¼ cup coarsely chopped nuts
¼ cup chopped maraschino cherries
1 envelope (1¼ ounces) low-calorie whipped
topping mix

Prepare Toasted Coconut Crust. Mix milk and lemon juice. Stir in fruit cocktail, nuts and cherries. Prepare topping mix as directed on package; fold into fruit cocktail mixture. Spread in pie crust. Refrigerate until set, 4 to 6 hours. Garnish with cherry halves and chopped nuts if desired.

TOASTED COCONUT CRUST

Heat oven to 325°. Spread 3 tablespoons butter or margarine, softened, on bottom and side of 9-inch pie plate. Press 1 can (3½ ounces) flaked coconut firmly and evenly against bottom and side of plate. Bake until golden brown, 15 to 20 minutes. Cool.

Stir ¼ cup grenadine syrup and 2 teaspoons lemon juice into cornstarch mixture.

Pour the grenadine mixture evenly on the blueberries in pie shell; refrigerate.

Blueberry Grenadine Pie

- 1 package (11 ounces) pie crust mix
- 2 cups fresh blueberries
- ½ cup sugar
- 1 tablespoon plus 2 teaspoons cornstarch
- ¼ teaspoon salt
- ¼ teaspoon ground cinnamon
- ¾ cup water
- ¼ cup grenadine syrup
- 2 teaspoons lemon juice
- ½ cup chilled whipping cream
- 1 tablespoon sugar

Bake 9-inch pie shell as directed on pie crust mix package. Cool. Place blueberries in pie shell. Blend ½ cup sugar, the cornstarch, salt and cinnamon in saucepan. Stir in water. Heat to boiling, stirring constantly. Boil and stir 1 minute. Stir in grenadine syrup and lemon juice. Pour on blueberries in pie shell. Refrigerate.

Beat whipping cream and 1 tablespoon sugar in chilled small mixer bowl until stiff. Top pie with whipped cream.

Melon Alaska Pie

1 package (11 ounces) pie crust mix
1 quart vanilla or peach ice cream, slightly
  softened
4 egg whites
¼ teaspoon cream of tartar
½ cup sugar
2 cups honeydew and/or cantaloupe balls*

Bake 9-inch pie shell as directed on pie crust mix package. Cool. Pack ice cream carefully into pie shell. Freeze until firm, at least 8 hours.

Ten minutes before serving, heat oven to 500°. Beat egg whites and cream of tartar until foamy. Beat in sugar gradually until meringue is stiff and glossy. Arrange fruit on ice cream; top with meringue, sealing to edge of crust. Bake until meringue is light brown, about 3 minutes.

*2 cups sliced nectarines, peaches, strawberries or blueberries can be substituted for the honeydew and cantaloupe balls.

Pack the slightly softened ice cream into the pie shell.

Use a melon baller to scoop uniform balls from melons.

Spread ice cream to edge of the Gingersnap Crust.

Swirl pumpkin mixture over the ice cream layer.

Frosty Pumpkin Pie

Gingersnap Crust (right)
1 cup mashed cooked pumpkin
¼ cup packed brown sugar
1 teaspoon aromatic bitters
½ teaspoon salt
½ teaspoon ground ginger
¼ teaspoon ground nutmeg
¼ teaspoon ground cinnamon
1 carton (4½ ounces) frozen whipped
   topping, thawed
1 pint butter pecan ice cream, slightly
   softened
2 tablespoons chopped pecans

Bake Gingersnap Crust; cool. Mix pumpkin, brown sugar, bitters, salt, ginger, nutmeg and cinnamon. Fold whipped topping into pumpkin mixture. Spoon ice cream into Gingersnap Crust; spread to edge of crust. Swirl pumpkin mixture over ice cream. Freeze uncovered at least 3 hours.

Let stand at room temperature 15 minutes before serving. Sprinkle pecans in circle on pie.

GINGERSNAP CRUST

Heat oven to 350°. Mix 1½ cups gingersnap crumbs and ¼ cup butter or margarine, melted. Press firmly and evenly against bottom and side of 9-inch pie plate. Bake 10 minutes.

Tangy Mince Cream Pie

2 cups regular granola, crushed
¼ cup butter or margarine, melted
2 tablespoons sugar
2 packages (8 ounces each) cream cheese,
    softened
2 eggs
¾ cup sugar
2 teaspoons vanilla
½ teaspoon grated lemon peel
  Whipped topping
  Mincemeat Sauce (below)

Heat oven to 350°. Mix granola, butter and 2 tablespoons
sugar. Press mixture firmly and evenly against bottom and
side of 9-inch pie plate. Bake until golden brown, 6 to 8
minutes.

Beat cream cheese slightly. Add eggs, ¾ cup sugar, the
vanilla and lemon peel; beat until light and fluffy. Pour into
crust. Bake until center is firm, about 25 minutes. Cool to
room temperature. Refrigerate at least 4 hours. Top with
whipped topping and serve with Mincemeat Sauce.

MINCEMEAT SAUCE

Blend 2 teaspoons cornstarch and 1 cup cranberry juice or
port in 1-quart saucepan. Heat to boiling. Boil and stir 1
minute; remove from heat. Stir in 1 cup prepared mincemeat. Serve warm or cool.

Timing Tip: If you want to serve at different times, Tangy
Mince Cream Pie and Mincemeat Sauce will hold cov-
ered in refrigerator up to 48 hours.

Prune Whip Pie

Cinnamon Pie Shell (below)
2 cups miniature marshmallows
½ cup hot water
½ teaspoon instant coffee
1½ cups chopped cooked prunes
1 tablespoon lemon juice
⅛ teaspoon salt
2 envelopes (1¼ ounces each) low-calorie
 whipped topping mix

Prepare Cinnamon Pie Shell. Heat marshmallows, water and coffee over low heat, stirring constantly, until marshmallows are melted, about 3 minutes. Refrigerate 30 minutes.

Reserve ¼ cup of the prunes. Stir remaining prunes, the lemon juice and salt into marshmallow mixture. Prepare 1 envelope whipped topping mix as directed on package; fold into prune mixture. Spread in pie shell. Refrigerate until set, about 5 hours. Prepare remaining envelope whipped topping mix as directed on package; swirl over pie. Garnish with reserved prunes.

CINNAMON PIE SHELL

Bake pastry for 9-inch One-Crust Pie as directed on 1 package (11 ounces) pie crust sticks except—stir 1 teaspoon ground cinnamon into crumbled stick before adding water. Cool.

An 8-inch pie plate can be used to press the chocolate crumb mixture in a 9-inch pie plate.

Quickly stir the rum, ginger and instant coffee into the slightly softened ice cream.

Ginger-Rum Ice-Cream Pie

1½ cups chocolate wafer crumbs (about 25
    wafers)
¼ cup butter or margarine, melted
¼ cup rum or 1 teaspoon rum flavoring
2 tablespoons chopped crystallized ginger
    or ¼ teaspoon ground ginger
2 teaspoons instant coffee
1 quart vanilla ice cream, slightly softened

Heat oven to 350°. Mix crumbs and butter; reserve 1 to 2
tablespoons crumb mixture for topping. Press remaining
mixture firmly and evenly against bottom and side of 9-
inch pie plate. Bake until set, 8 to 10 minutes. Cool.

Stir rum, ginger and instant coffee into softened ice cream;
pour into pie shell. Freeze uncovered until firm, about 4
hours. Serve immediately or wrap, label and freeze up to
3 weeks.

■15 minutes before serving, unwrap pie and let stand at
room temperature for easier cutting.

Apricot-Almond Ice-Cream Pie: Substitute ½ cup diced
roasted almonds and ½ cup apricot preserves for the ginger and coffee.

Banana Ice-Cream Pie: Substitute 2 bananas, mashed, and
¼ cup frozen orange juice concentrate, thawed, for the
rum, ginger and coffee.

Confetti Cheese Pies

¾ cup butter or margarine, softened
2 cups all-purpose flour*
½ teaspoon salt
½ teaspoon grated lime or lemon peel
2 teaspoons cold water
1 package (8 ounces) cream cheese, softened
5 eggs, separated
1 can (14 ounces) sweetened condensed milk
⅓ cup lime or lemon juice
3 drops red food color
½ teaspoon grated lime or lemon peel
¼ teaspoon cream of tartar
2 cups frozen whipped topping, thawed
¼ cup confetti candy

Heat oven to 375°. Cut butter into flour, salt and ½ teaspoon lime peel with pastry blender; stir in water. Press pastry against bottoms and sides of two 9-inch pie plates.

Beat cream cheese, egg yolks, milk, lime juice and food color 2 minutes. Stir in ½ teaspoon lime peel. Beat egg whites and cream of tartar until stiff and glossy. Fold cheese mixture into egg whites; pour into crusts.

Bake until knife inserted in centers comes out clean, 20 to 25 minutes. Refrigerate 2 hours. Spread pies with whipped topping and sprinkle with confetti candy. 2 PIES.

*Do not use self-rising flour in this recipe.

Golden Glow Cheese Pies: Omit red food color and confetti candy. Garnish with canned apricot halves.

St. Patrick's Day Pies: Omit red food color and candy. Stir 2 drops each yellow and green food color into whipped topping. Garnish with whipped topping shamrocks.

For Golden Glow Cheese Pies, decorate with apricots.

For St. Patrick's Day Pies, decorate with shamrocks.

You need these ingredients to make the Pie Crust Mix. Yield is 9 cups of mix.

Fold the banana mixture, the whipped cream and ⅓ cup of the pecans into meringue.

Pie Crust Mix

Cut 3 cups shortening into 6 cups all-purpose flour* and 3 teaspoons salt until particles are size of small peas. Refrigerate in airtight container up to 1 month.   9 CUPS MIX.

*If using self-rising flour, omit salt.

Banana-Rum Pie

      2 to 3 tablespoons cold water
  1½ cups Pie Crust Mix (above)
      2 medium bananas, sliced
  ¼ to ½ cup light rum
  ¼ cup packed brown sugar
      1 envelope unflavored gelatin
      3 eggs, separated
      2 tablespoons banana liqueur
  ¼ cup granulated sugar
      1 cup chilled whipping cream, whipped
  ⅔ cup broken pecans

Heat oven to 475°. Sprinkle water, 1 tablespoon at a time, over Pie Crust Mix. Stir until moistened. Gather into a ball; roll 2 inches larger than inverted 9-inch pie plate on floured cloth-covered board. Ease into plate; trim edge 1 inch from rim. Fold and roll pastry under; flute. Prick thoroughly with fork. Bake 8 to 10 minutes. Cool.

Place bananas and rum in blender container. Cover and blend until smooth. Mix brown sugar and gelatin in saucepan. Beat in egg yolks; stir in ½ cup banana mixture. Cook, stirring constantly, until thickened. Stir in liqueur and remaining banana mixture. Refrigerate until mixture mounds slightly. Beat egg whites until foamy; beat in granulated sugar until stiff and glossy. Fold in banana mixture, cream and ⅓ cup pecans. Pour into pie shell; top with remaining pecans. Refrigerate until set, 2 to 3 hours.

Strawberry Flan Supreme

1 package (7.2 ounces) fluffy white frosting mix
1 cup chilled whipping cream
⅓ cup dairy sour cream
2 cups Pie Crust Mix (page 63)
½ cup sugar
½ cup milk
2 eggs
1 teaspoon baking powder
1 teaspoon vanilla
1 pint strawberries, sliced
Mint sprigs

Mix frosting mix, whipping cream and sour cream. Cover and refrigerate at least 1 hour.

Heat oven to 350°. Grease and flour 4-cup flan pan. Beat Pie Crust Mix, sugar, milk, eggs, baking powder and vanilla on low speed, scraping bowl constantly, 30 seconds. Beat on medium speed, scraping bowl occasionally, 2 minutes; pour into pan. Bake until wooden pick inserted in center comes out clean, 20 to 25 minutes. Cool 5 minutes. Invert on wire rack; remove pan. Cool completely.

Stir frosting mixture; beat until stiff. Reserve ½ cup of the strawberries; fold remaining strawberries into frosting mixture. Spread in flan shell. Garnish with reserved strawberries and the mint sprigs.

A B C D E F